Shattering Barriers

By Josh Knipple

Publisher:

Abba Father Media Inc.

AbbaFatherMedia.com

1-928531671

Dedication

I dedicate this book to my dad Terry for teaching me to wake up each day and say, “God, how can you use me today?”

Table of Contents

Dedication *3*

Table of Contents *4*

Introduction *6*

Shattering Barriers *6*

Chapter 1 .... *8*

Therefore!!! *8*

Chapter 2 .... *13*

Value *13*

Chapter 3 .... *17*

Who Is Jesus To You? *17*

Chapter 4 .... *23*

Repent, Change, Do a 180, Go and Sin No More. *23*

Chapter 5 .... *28*

God's Unfathomable Faithfulness, by Christa *28*

Chapter 6 .... *30*

Christa Watson's Testimony *30*

Chapter 7 .... *32*

Life through Death-- Truly *32*

Chapter 8 .... *36*

Lost *36*

Chapter 9 .... *41*

Go! Are You Willing? *41*

Chapter 10 .... *45*

ShowTime *45*

Chapter 11 .... *49*

A Dangerous Prayer, a Serious Calling *49*

Bibliography *55*

Web Sites: *55*

About The Author *56*

Introduction

Shattering Barriers

Outside the walls of church, hanging out with sinners, that is exactly where Christ went. To the outcasts, the broken, the beat up, the homeless and the sick. It is also what got Him in trouble with the religious of the day. Mark 2:16-17. When the Scribes and the Pharisees saw that He was eating with the sinners and tax collectors, they said to His disciples, "Why is He eating and drinking with tax collectors and sinners?" Hearing this, Jesus said to them, "It is not those who are healthy who need a physician, but those who are sick; I did not come to call the righteous, but sinners." Are we willing to go where Jesus would go or are we worried what the religious will think that we seclude ourselves from the world and form our own little Christian bubble? Let's be honest we have gotten very good at preaching to those who have already heard instead of taking the gospel to the unreached. It is time we expand our view and actually start caring about our dying neighbors, instead of waiting for them to come in the church. How about we be the church and take the name of Christ to them! Let's get outside the walls. "God open my eyes to those around me who need to hear your truth."

My hope with this book, Shattering Barriers, is that I would present to you stories about Jesus working outside the walls of church in ways we would not normally look at and that through them hearts would be convicted. With each chapter I will try and break down a story of God working and then add practical everyday ways to apply it to our own personal lives. My prayer is that as you read this book you take an honest look at your own heart and ask God to change you in ways He needs to for His Glory to shine through.

Chapter 1

Therefore!!!

One small word changed my life, my outlook, and the way I approach people and ministry! A word that I read over and most of the time and didn't really think about. Upon further review it has major meaning. The simple word is therefore as found is 2 Corinthians 4:13. "It is written, I believed and THEREFORE I have spoken. Since we have that same spirit of faith, we also believe and THEREFORE speak." At first it may not seem that important, but let's really look at this. Therefore can be defined; "as a result of," or "due to the fact," or "for the reason of." So when Paul is writing these words he is stating because he believes he is compelled to speak!

If you notice he starts out with the word I believe. It is personal. As I stated earlier faith is a personal thing. You have to figure out what you believe on your own. Not what your parents believe or your pastor tells you, or even what I am telling you. What do you believe? This is foundational here.

Let's start out with a few simple questions to really think about. First, do you believe that Jesus is the way to God, the one and only as stated in John 14:6? Second, do you believe that He changes lives? Is He the greatest Gift one could ever receive? Finally, do you believe in the existence of hell? I know, no one likes to talk about the existence of hell, but you have to ask yourself now, do you believe in the reality of separation from God for eternity?

Many of you probably answered yes to all those questions. You at least shook your head going of course, “I believe those things.” Well, if you said that then Paul is challenging you here to speak! The problem is many of us have become so comfortable with the world.

It is uncomfortable for us to speak about our faith. We don’t want to cause any controversy or stir things up so we translate that verse to say, “I believe, but I am going to keep it to myself.” “I believe, but it is the Pastors job to speak.” “I believe but?” We have all kind of excuses as to why we don’t share this belief. If we truly believe then we are called to speak! Some of you are already probably disagreeing with me, but hear me out.

Think of it this way. Maybe some of you reading this have a kid already or you can say you want to have kids one day. Think of that child. One day you notice he starts having bruises appear all over him and you notice a significant drop in weight. His figure begins to slowly change and as a parent you start to get concerned. You begin to take him to the doctors in the area and they cannot figure out what is wrong. They are taking tests like crazy, but cannot quite figure out what is causing your sons pain. Then you hear of a doctor in California who knows the answer. He has the cure 100 percent guaranteed! You are ecstatic and begin to tell your child everything is going to be okay! You do everything you can to get your kid there and finally when the day arrives, the doctor looks at you and says, "Yes I have the cure, but because it is controversial, I can't help you!" You are heartbroken, upset, angry, and screaming, "tell me, please!"

It may seem a bit extreme, but here is the reality. You and I am the doctor with the cure. The sickness is what we know as sin. People all around us, including friends and family are dying on the inside, seeking that answer that we have in Christ. He is a 100 percent guaranteed cure for their sin. He can give them life, hope, a future, and freedom from that sickness.

Where it is easier for us to keep our mouths shut instead of telling the world that Jesus saves, because we might be rejected, cause a stir or get rejected. Let's be honest. We are living in a desperate time with people all around us crying out for help. Will we stand up and tell them that He is what they need and are looking for, or continue to keep silent?

Okay, another way to look at it. Think back to last Christmas. Remember that one amazing gift you got you could not wait to tell your friends about. I don't know about you, but Christmas is a major thing for me. I remember as a kid starting to come up with my wish in April for the following Christmas. You research, you look up things, and you go through the Toys R Us catalog over and over and figure out exactly what you want. You dream about it, you hope for it, and then Christmas day comes around and you get it! You are so excited and if you are anything like me you can't wait to open it up and start using it. Always, showing it off to friends and family, of course! Or maybe it is your first car. Even if it was a piece of junk you were 16 and you couldn't wait to go pick up the guys and go cruising. You were excited and had to talk about it and show it off.

Now going back to the question, is Jesus the greatest gift you could ever receive? If you answered yes then how in the world do we keep silent about Him? We show off our toys and talk about our car, but we keep silent about him? It would be like receiving that favorite toy Christmas day and throwing it in the closet, hiding it away. Or just leaving that car parked in the garage to collect dust. Absolutely not! We talk about them, we show them off! Why? They are important to us. Yet Jesus, our so called best gift we could receive or give, we hide away. Are you starting to get my drift?

We are way off when it comes to our faith. We can sit and talk sports, the weather, the latest gossip, about the new girl in church, but the one conversation that might actually change eternity we keep silent about. The one conversation that will save their soul, that could change all of eternity, we are ashamed of. Something is out of whack. No More. Paul challenges us to speak up. I believe therefore I speak! We can no longer walk around with our heads down ashamed of what we say we believe. We desire to see the world changed for Christ then it is time we open our mouths. Peter and John put it this way in Acts 4:20, "You cannot keep us silent about what we know is true." Even facing imprisonment and death they had the faith to say you cannot silence my message! I know how important it is. Kill me if you want, but you will not keep me silent. How about you?

Now I know some of you may be sitting here reading and saying, "well Josh my actions speak for me." I will be the first to say awesome, because I do believe our actions speak louder than words, but I have to ask the question, "does anyone notice anything different or is that just your way to justify not speaking?" Think about it. If your actions are speaking then I applaud you and tell you to keep it up, just as Saint Francis said, "preach the Gospel always, if necessary use words!" Either way I challenge you in saying, it is time we open our mouths and allow our actions to bring hope to a dying world in need of a Savior!

"I BELIEVE AND THEREFORE I SPEAK!"

Chapter 2

Value

Value! An important word! In life, it is something everyone desires. Whether you term it as self- worth, self confidence, achievement, or however else, it is something we all want to feel. From our parents, our peers, co-workers, friends, we all want to feel like we have a purpose in life and meaning to others. Yet it is also one of the biggest struggles people deal with.

This is one of the biggest lessons I have learned over the past few years and one of the main things I have seen Jesus teach me about in ministry. When I was in high school, as many of you reading can probably admit to, we place people into categories to determine their worth. The Athletes, the cheerleaders, those in band, the brains, the haves and the have not's, the popular, the dateable, the untouchables, and the list goes on and on. It is sad though how we do it. Depending on the category you're in, determines your worth and value to others. Coaches tell you that you are just not big enough or fast enough. Teachers tell you that you are just not smart enough. Even your parents tell you that you are just never going to amount to anything in life. Kids go home hearing these statements and begin to believe them and feel that they have no self-worth. It is crazy how kids, because of statements like these now contemplate suicide. Some struggle with cutting and depression. Then in turn, this leads them into drinking and drugs just as an escape.

Then to make matters worse, media promotes the idea that the perfect body and physical appearance is what you need to get anywhere in life. You may think I am over exaggerating this fact. Next time you go to the store look at how many magazines are about the perfect body or how to have those six pack abs. Magazines cover the top one hundred beautiful people and so on. TV commercials do the same exact thing with their before and after pills, promoting that true happiness is found in a body type.

What is crazy is that even in churches we have bought into the same lies. A guest comes walking in the church door, someone popular and everyone flocks to them making sure they feel welcomed. Following right behind them is a homeless guy who maybe doesn't smell the best and we turn and walk the other way. Who are we showing that they have value? Truly think about this idea.

God created each and every one of us differently. Give thanks. Our world would be pretty dang boring if we all looked and acted exactly the same. Scripture tells us in Psalms 139 that he knitted each and every one of us together before we were even born. So who are we to judge if a person has value or not based on how they look.

Jesus really hit me hard with this truth a few years ago at the skate park. I will never forget. It was a Tuesday night at the local outdoor park and I saw one of the kids sneak away by him-self and sit down by a tree and just start balling. At the time I thought that it was kind of strange. I went over to find out what was going on with him. I started asking the basic questions. “Did you get hurt or is someone picking on you?” Nope. He went on to explain to me that, because of the medication he is on every day that he breaks down emotionally three to four times a day uncontrollably. He then went on to tell me how hard it is in school because of his crying spells. My heart began to break for him. I tried to imagine what that must be like getting picked on over something you cannot control. It was in that moment Jesus began to whisper in my ear, "I love that kid as much as I love you."

I have learned that when Jesus wants to get your attention about something He will continue to teach you in His own small ways. It wasn't long after that skate park experience that I had a girl show up to the skate park. She was fifteen years old and I asked her how her week was going. She proceeded to roll up her sleeves and show me the slice marks from cutting. She said, "How does it look like it is going?" As I got to hear more of her story I found out that she cuts because of all the things that are said about her at school and at home. She said because she is Goth. Again my heart broke. In that moment I heard Jesus whispering to my heart, "I died for her." From those two moments on, God has continued to show me and whisper to me those same statements. Through ministering to more and more broken down people, who the world might call wash-ups, Jesus continues to say, "They're of value to me and they should be of value to you!"

Think about this a second, you are the only person alive on the face of the earth, just you and your sin. What if I told you that Jesus would have came and died just for you to show you His love? Amazing, right? Now that is love. He has value in you! Same goes for every other person out there. Every kid, no matter their background, their home situation, the class they fit into and their looks. Jesus died for them as much as He did for you and me. Jesus loves them just the same.

Maybe you are reading this now questioning your existence. You have been beat up at school and told some pretty hurtful things that no one ever deserves to hear. Trust me in this. JESUS LOVES YOU and he has a plan and purpose for you. Maybe as you're reading this, your heart is being convicted. If you're going to be honest you're the one doing the judging. Maybe you need to open your heart up to others and see them as a treasure in Christ's eyes.

As believers we need to start seeing people, each and every one as valuable in Christ's eyes. This makes them valuable in our eyes also. We are all in the same grouping. We're sinners in need of a Savior. Created by God in his image! Let's start seeing each-other all the same way.

James 2: 2-4, "Suppose a man comes into your meeting wearing a gold ring and fine clothes and a poor man in filthy old clothes also comes in. If you show special attention to the man wearing fine clothes and say, "Here's a good seat for you," but say to the poor man, "You stand there" or "Sit on the floor by my feet," have you not discriminated among yourselves and become judges with evil thoughts?

Chapter 3

Who Is Jesus To You?

To know where to start, honestly still not a clue. This book has been five years in the making with a lot of thought, a lot of learning and a lot of study. It is going to be a collection of thoughts and a collection of heartfelt stories with conviction. It is going to contain honesty. I probably will upset a few people. I hopefully will make you laugh at times. Above all I hope by writing this book it will serve as a wakeup call to many of us who want to take faith seriously!

I am not going to try and pretend that I have figured everything out when it comes to faith. I am still learning a lot of lessons myself. One thing God has taught me is that we need to share what we are learning with others. Over the past few years God has taught me within the church, through being a pastor. He has taught me what it means to do outreach at a skate park. He has taught me what it means to love the untouchables at a homeless and broken dinner in town. He has taught me what it means to just be real with people and how building relationships with people is one of the most important things there is in this world. Ministry has taught me some of the goods of faith and also some of the downfalls. None of this would be possible without Christ. Jesus is the one and only, and the reason behind this book. This book would not be possible if it were not for him changing my heart. He is in the midst of each and every story. Enjoy!

I hope that as I write these stories they will challenge your heart, convict and maybe break your heart as you read. I hope to see God change people one person at a time.

I have many different ways I've thought about starting this book. I thought about opening with a few zinger stories that might cut to the heart. Maybe even a one liner or two to get you laughing. Maybe even an opening paragraph that makes you think and go man this is going to be a good book making you not to want to put it down. Honestly, after prayer and a lot of blank thoughts that I kept trying to come up with, God gave me this opening message. Start with me!!! It was like a light bulb went off in my head. What a concept! Start a Christian book off talking about Jesus and who He is. As you will find out I am pretty simple minded so you can just imagine me sitting there staring up in space going hum, what should I say? "God what do you want?" Hoping words would just start appearing. Yeah it didn't happen that way, but like I said He did give me this thought to start with. Talk about Jesus! Who is He?

Let's start out from the very beginning. Probably the most important question you need to ask yourself. Who is Jesus to you? Matthew 16 sets up a perfect scene for this question. First off Jesus asks a simple question, "Who do others say that I am?" But then he cuts straight to the chase, right to the heart of the matter, by asking, "Now who do you say that I am?" He was blunt! Let's be honest, we never get past the first question. "Who do others say Jesus is?" We give answers based on what we have heard.

Maybe what our pastor has told us. Maybe what our parents told us. Let's be honest, maybe all we have ever thought about Jesus and who He is to us, is from a song lyric or a hymn we have heard or sung in church. The disciples answered, some say you are a prophet. Others say you could be Elijah or Jeremiah. Some even called Him John the Baptist. These are answers of what they had heard about Him. But He is so much more. But what if that is all we ever know of Jesus? We will never think for ourselves about who He is to us.

A few years back I witnessed this firsthand. I was speaking at a local youth group doing a message on this exact passage. I thought it would be a great way to challenge some of the kids there by having them stand up and share personal experiences about who Christ is and what He means to them. I was fired up about it and I couldn't wait to hear the answers. Let me just say this, when you ask youth to share in front and you give them a microphone you never know what you are going to get. So kids at first were hesitant to come forward, but slowly they began. There answers caught me off guard. At first I was happy that kids were stepping up at all so I put a smile on my face and just kept listening, "He is my shepherd, He is my joy and He is my light." All great answers, but as they were speaking I noticed that a lot of the answers were just answers they had heard from others and not a personal answer. I wanted to stand up and scream, "CHURCH ANSWERS," think for your-self!"

At that point God got a hold of me and slapped me around, because the next kid who got up was a seventeen year old skater who floored me with his answer. He started out by saying, "I am not even sure if I am allowed to say this in church, but you told me to be real so here it goes." "Jesus to me is like that first dip of Copenhagen I get in the morning." "He is what gets me going and brings me joy." "The days I do not have Him in my life are obvious." "I am grumpy, angry and start feeling sick." "He is my happiness". Whoa, wait, did you hear that? This kid just compared Jesus to chew. Now I pray that you do not close the book already, because this is a real answer. Think about it, this kid was being straight-up when talking about who Jesus was to him. An addiction! He needs him every day! Wow! What an answer! At that point, let me tell you it got real! Kids began thinking about who Jesus truly was to them. No more sugar coating, happy go lucky answers. Straight forward brutal honesty!

The other answer I will never forget that day was from one of our leaders. She was twenty at the time and when she started I knew it was going to be heartfelt, because as soon as she grabbed the microphone she started to sob. She stated, "Jesus is my knight in shining armor. " At the time I wasn't sure where she was headed and honestly I was thinking she was going to tell us how God had told her to be single or something like that. Again, as soon as my thoughts started being cynical God took her words and shook my world. She went on to share the story of how she had been engaged.

Her fiancée had proposed to her two weeks before he got deployed. When he was overseas, he was one of our men who didn't make it back home.

She was devastated that the man of her dreams was gone, but that Jesus is what got her through that time. He truly was her knight when she needed one most! Honesty! If you are not moved by this you should check yourself for a pulse. I share those two stories as examples of real life honesty of who Jesus is. It made me think. That morning was a life change for me. Did I have my own personal answer or was I just going off what others had told me?

Picture this. You are sitting in your room all alone. Silence around you, no one else there. All of a sudden there is a light in your doorway and it is coming closer to you. At once you realize it is Him, Jesus, the one and only Savior. He starts out by saying, "do not be afraid, I just want to talk." I do not know about you, but even if He says do not be afraid I still may have a little bit of a wet spot on my bed. Just saying! If you would be honest, you probably would also! Here you are bracing yourself as the King of Kings says, hey let's talk. He is going to call you out on your sin from last week, or from yesterday. He is going to work a miracle in front of you, maybe turn your glass of water into wine? What could it be that He wants? Nonchalantly He asks you a question, "Who am I to you?" Could you answer? What would you say?

Would you give Him a church answer you have heard over and over? Is He personal to you? When Jesus asks His disciples this question in verse 16, Peter gives us a response. "You are the Messiah, the Son of the Living God." Now verse 17 is just as important to realize when looking at this story, because it is Jesus responding, "Blessed are you

Simon, for this was not revealed to you by flesh and blood, but by my Father in Heaven. " Did you catch that? This was not revealed to you by man, but by God. This was not a church answer that you heard in a song, but this was something that God Himself has shown to you. Why this is so important is that it shows us that God Himself will reveal to us what He wants us to know. We are all going to see Christ differently and hopefully have different answers that are personal answers of who Christ is to us.

Remember that those answers of who Christ is are being revealed from above. Think of it this way. If I called on a leader of the church up to the front and said, "Okay who is this man to you?" Describe Him. We would all have different answers. His wife and kids would describe Him differently than a co-worker would or maybe some of his friends. Why? They have all experienced this man differently. This is the same thing when it comes to knowing Christ. It is a beautiful thing. We will all know and experience Christ differently. God will reveal different things about who Christ is to each of us through different stories and experiences. One thing I would hope and pray that we would all have in common would be the first answer that came to my mind. Jesus, you are my Savior and Lord. Is He that to you? That is going to be foundational to this book. I want you to put this book down, open up your Bible and look at Matthew 16:13-17. Study it. And ask yourself, "Who Is Christ to you?"

Chapter 4

Repent, Change, Do a 180, Go and Sin No More

Jesus calls us to a crazy, radical life change. The word change, we want nothing to do with. We have become very comfortable with our lives and very content with whom we are. Life change takes work. Change isn't always fun. Sometimes it hurts. Think about it, moving, rearranging, changing jobs, breaking up, all these things take work. I'll be honest; I am a creature of habit. In the morning I have a set routine. I wake-up, get coffee, watch at least one episode of Sports Center, and don't talk to anyone if possible. After that I take a shower, brush my teeth and then start my day. When even that schedule gets thrown off it takes a little time to adjust. It may seem you need to seriously think about your life. We all have certain things in our lives we have been accustomed to and we have become content with. Here is the thing. Jesus calls us to change.

In Christian terms; Repent! Here is the problem. As we do not like change in our lives and have become so comfortable with a way of living, we also have become comfortable with the sin in our lives. At first there may have been some conviction about it but instead of changing we instead let it become part of our daily lives. It has become part of what we know and do on a daily basis without even thinking about it or the consequences to it. We get to the point that we just accept It because it would be harder to change than to actually deal with it. We use the excuse, "well that is what God's grace is all about." But as Paul writes in Romans 6, "Shall we continue sinning so that His grace may abound more.

Absolutely Not! But that is the mindset many have adopted and grown to know. Herein lays the problem. Jesus calls us to holiness.

We discussed in Chapter 1, who is Christ to you? Now let's take that a little bit further. Is He enough to you to change your life? Is He enough to change your way? Is He enough to leave your life of sin behind? Is Jesus that kind of reason for you to change?

Let's look at a story in scripture here real quick. (John 8) At dawn He appeared again in the temple courts; where all the people gathered around Him, and He sat down to teach them. The teachers of the law and the Pharisees brought in a woman caught in adultery. They made her stand before the group and said to Jesus, "Teacher, this woman was caught in the act of adultery. In the Law Moses commanded us to stone such women. Now what do you say?" They were using this question as a trap, in-order to have a basis for accusing Him. Jesus bent down and started to write on the ground with His finger. When they kept on questioning Him, He straightened up and said to them, "Let any one of you who is without sin be the first to throw a stone at her." Again He stooped down and wrote on the ground. At this, those who heard began to go away one at a time, the older ones first, until only Jesus was left, with the woman still standing there. Jesus straightened up and asked her, "Woman, where are they? Has no one condemned you?"

"No one, sir," she said. "Then neither do I condemn you," Jesus declared. "Go now and leave your life of sin."

Okay, let's start off with this thought. Put

yourself in this woman's shoes. She was caught in the act, drug out into public, humiliated and deserving death. Guilty as charged. Okay a little oversimplified. Really think about this. Here she is caught in her life of sin and brought before the religious people of the day. As she is standing there she hears them say, "Teacher in the law of Moses it is commanded that she is to be stoned." Can you imagine if that was you hearing those words? You have just been told that because of your acts you deserve death, and not just death but death by stoning. We do not have the exact way in which someone was stoned during this time but some of the earliest records describe it as a hole was dug about waist deep. The person was placed inside and then the declaring judge would take the first stone, about tangerine size, and throw it at the condemned. After his stone was thrown, the mob would join in until the person was declared dead.

I don't know about you but at that point, I would be falling to me knees begging for mercy and grace. I am sure that morning, when the woman chose to commit adultery the last thing she thought was that she would be caught facing her punishment. But wait. Instead of giving in to the Pharisees demand, Jesus does something peculiar. He bends over and starts writing in the sand. We are not really sure what was written in the sand that day, but many have said that He began to write the sins of the Pharisees themselves. Whatever it was, it was enough for the Pharisees to all walk away themselves. What a turn of events. Can you imagine? Maybe He wrote; lust, anger, pride, arrogance, greed, envy, murder. John goes onto to say the Pharisees began to walk away one at a time, the oldest first until none remained. At this moment Jesus stands up and asks her, "Where are your condemners?" They're all gone. Then His great words of forgiveness, "then neither do I condemn you!" Wait, What? "I was just sentenced to die a moment ago and now you are telling me no condemnation." Yes, that is exactly what He is saying. Here is the kicker. This next simple statement we leave out many times, or overlook. Is the statement, "NOW GO AND SIN NO MORE!" This is a life change. I have forgiven you and now I want you to change. Repent. Leave this life you have known behind. He gives her the choice to change.

I would love to sit here and tell you that at that moment she went home and told all her family and friends what just took place and that the entire village came to Christ because of her and her testimony. We don't have any record of that. I would love to tell you that her life was never the same and she can always look back to that moment and those words "go and sin no more," and she cleaned her life up and was altered forever. What a miraculous story that would turn out to be. But we don't have record of that. All we can do is imagine and hope that she changed that day.

Here is the thing though. We have that choice in our own lives. We all can put ourselves in her shoes, deserving of death due to our sin. She was caught in the act before Jesus and He offered forgiveness and hope. Standing up, picking us up now go and leave you life of sin." What will we do? Will we change? Will we take His words to heart? Will we realize the magnitude of what He is offering us? A fresh start! Deserving death but being offered life. Deserving wrath but being shown grace. He gives us the choice. What will you do with it?

Will you change? Will you take it and share your story to others of the difference Jesus made in your life? Will you be grateful for Him saving you?

Or will you continue right as you are?

The choice is yours.

Chapter 5

God's Unfathomable Faithfulness, by Christa

I had a lot of questions when I felt God leading me from Longview Texas to Australia as a Missionary with Youth with a Mission, YWAM. My main question was how I would raise the ten Thousand dollars I needed in-order to go and stay? God told me through His word to just trust Him. I did. It came to my first payment and I had no money. I was in college part-time and paying for a new car all on a non-profit salary. At this time, I worked at a rescue mission, a Christian homeless Shelter, and often ate meals at the shelter to save money for my trip. I even traded my new car for my sisters older paid off car. Still when it came time I had no money.

You see, God told me He would provide and He would get the glory. It wouldn't be anything I worked for, but I was to have faith. I had to pay in two hundred dollars. I did not have it but God gave me peace. The day before it was due a homeless man and his case worker walked in my office and the homeless man handed me two hundred dollars! No one knew how much money I needed, I never told anyone. I refused it at first. I mean how could I take money from someone in need? His case manager, my co-worker, looked at me and said "you let him do what the Lord put on his heart." He provided money from family, friends and people I didn't even know. Fast forward six months. I just finished my discipleship training school with YWAM. I had seen God move in mighty ways in Australia, London, and Nepal. I saw His power, as we called out over people in the name of Jesus, to be healed and to be freed from demons. I felt the Holy Spirit free me of past hurts and regrets. At the end of it all, I was called back to continue learning with YWAM in their school for media. It would cost ten thousand dollars and I had absolutely zero dollars. With only two weeks left to raise the money and it was Christmas time, the hardest time to fundraise.

Again I sat in Longview Texas, this time at a red light and asked in prayer," Dad, could you just provide the money and give me peace?" God overwhelmed me with peace and I drove to volunteer at the rescue mission I had worked at before. An hour later I got a call from my earthly father saying he had a friend that wanted to donate eighteen thousand dollars to my mission funds! Once again God proved His faithfulness and I went back to Australia. I am currently making an evangelical film for the Limbu people in Nepal. A movie expected to reach a group of people who have been lost and unreached to this point. Oh and because I was provided for in abundance, I was able to obey God in helping financially some of my other teammates go to Nepal as well. God is so good!

Chapter 6

Christa Watson's Testimony

Homesickness is a feeling I have come by rarely in my many years of being away from home, but as I sit in a puddle of sweat in Nepal my heart longs for the familiarity of home and the comfort of all that comes with it. You see at home I know the language, the culture, and the way of life. I know what is offensive and what's not. I make decisions based on what is good for me in that moment. It sounds selfish as I write this all down, but my heart longs to be free of having to try so hard just to say hello.

With that said this is my calling, a calling, to the nations. People look at my life and turn up their noses, because I am twenty-seven years old, not married or even close to it. No kids. No stability as far as the world is concerned. No money, besides what the Lord provides. Others look at me and wish they could have this life. It would be hard for them. Some see me as a wanderer without direction. I won't lie. It is appealing to me at times to have ministry in one place with a husband and maybe a kid or two. Me being able to go to a local church, I could be a Sunday school teacher and settled down in one place, without living out of a bag. I don't know and often don't agree with or even like. I am challenged by them. I go in and out of conveniences, such as electricity, toilets, clean water and culture shock. I am told to just get over it, because it is for Jesus. I have spent the last six months sick from the last time I was in Nepal. I am not sure of when the sickness will leave. Looking at this from this view I began to demand my rights before God and He reminded me of His rights. Being an American Citizen, rights are huge to me! What about my rights as a heavenly citizen? Jesus did lay down all His rights to die on a cross for me! He is God, but forever gave up His Godly form to be man, so that I could enter a place of grace and forgiveness with the father. You see I am just one of the billions of people God has called and no matter how uncomfortable I am I have a higher calling than my own happiness. I have an urgency to show the light of Jesus to the world. I have seen demons flee people at the sound of the name of Jesus and people healed with the same power of this name. I have seen relationships and lives restored.

I have watched peace fill faces that one would have given up hope on. I am reminded of the sinner that I am and how only by Christ's kindness am I even alive. Hallelujah that I have to do without and learn to love. This makes me fall in love with my Jesus so much more and at the end of my life all I long to hear is good job my good and faithful servant. I have a lot of work to do to get to this point, but I am trusting in faith that my God has the best plan for my life. I choose to lay down my rights for the cross, because I know the cross gives life everlasting and true joy! Thank God for the empty grave. The cross leads to life! God makes me smile!

Chapter 7

Life through Death-- Truly

To be honest as I begin to write this and go back to the night it happened, tears are literally coming to my eyes. But as you read it and start to really consider it, I have a feeling many of you will be grabbing tissues by the end of the chapter. Call me a softy if you want but this chapter truly exemplifies God's love for you in the most real way I have ever known.

As a pastor I have to do hospital calls at times, which to be honest are very uncomfortable to me. Many times I do not know what to say in the least and at times feel very inadequate as a pastor. Over the years I have had to make my share of them. My dad is also a pastor so at times we will tag-team hospital calls. This is one of those stories.

It happened this past summer. One of the members of my father's church was on vacation in Myrtle Beach enjoying time with his family. He, his wife and his two kids playing in the ocean like so many of us do when the unthinkable happened. A wave hit him the wrong way and knocked him into the surf. When he became conscious he couldn't move. On this tragic day, he broke his neck. Still completely alert, but just unable to move. They took him to the hospital in South Carolina and got him stabilized but delivered the news that he would never walk again and that his life was in serious jeopardy. A few weeks go by and they chose to transport him back to Johnstown to continue his care, but not giving him much hope at all. He is now in a hospital and being given pain meds for all the pain he is going through. He can whisper and read lips, but as days go on things begin to take a turn for the worse. The doctors come in and tell him that because of his condition he's developing a very serious infection.

His family continues to try and be strong and stand by his side even though they are breaking on the inside seeing their husband and dad in this state. Here is where my dad and I come into the picture. Over the next month or so my dad would spend hours at the hospital talking to him and sharing the hope of Jesus with him even in the state he was in. When he was in pain at night my dad would tell him to just whisper the name Jesus to calm him down. This is nothing magical, or some secret amazing prayer, just crying out to Jesus.

I would love to sit here and give you a fairy tale ending about this story and that this man is now at home with his family but sometimes God's greatest gifts truly are unanswered prayers. After about a month being back in town the doctors came in and shared the news that he had two options at this point: to go in and fuse his neck completely together so that they could roll him over to clear the infection, or to give him medication to make him comfortable until he passed. Talk about heartbreaking news and a long couple of days of heartbreak for the family. He chose the latter option.

Here is where the story gets crazy. He literally was given the option of when he wanted to go. The only thing keeping him alive at this point was the machines. Even though totally conscious and able to communicate with us the entire rest of his body had shut down. So over the next couple days he got to spend his final moments making things right with family members, saying a final goodbye to friends and even causing all of us in the family to laugh. But the one thing I will never forget is him saying to us, "don't hold on to me, I am going to a better place where my pain will be gone and I will be healed with my savior." During this time he also chose that his organs could be used. He wanted to donate them so that through his death others could live.

Here he was, the day had come and the family gathered all around. You would think there would be crying but instead great joy. He laid there making jokes and talked Notre Dame Football. Then the organ donation doctor came in the room and began to share with the family where his organs would be going and whose lives he would be saving. She shared with us how she had never in her career actually had the opportunity to share with the actual organ donor that kind of information. At that moment the tears began to flow, not of sorrow but of lives being changed by his sacrifice. Then the moment came when he was ready. He told his family how much he loved them and then made the decision that he wanted his brother to be the one to pull the plug. What an incredible scene to watch unfold. What a sacrifice he was choosing to make. He was giving up his life so that his family could move on and that others could live. Even the nurses all around were in tears. Incredible!

Really think about this a second. He could have chosen to stay alive and maybe hope to recover one day, but instead he knew what his future held by breathing his last breath. He would be healed and in doing so offer others life.

As I left the hospital that day I was shaking just thinking about what I had just witnessed. This was a man in his early fifties who said, "I am ready, let me go, so that others may live." If I was his brother could I have had the strength to pull the plug? If I was his family would I have been willing to let him go? Do I have the strength and faith that if placed in that situation I could have made that choice?

Then as I drove around town just sitting in amazement, God began to speak to my heart. He said, "Just as Ron laid down his life for others, so I also have laid down my life for all eternity. I gave up my one and only son in His prime so that you might live. He willingly gave up His breath so you could be made whole. You were in need of a new heart so he provided that for you on the cross. You were in need of clean hands and feet, so he washed them for you. You were in need of a new spirit, so He did that for you also. He willingly gave up His all so that you may live."

All I could do in that moment was return to the church, head to the prayer room and begin to sing at the top of my lungs over and over, "Oh, How he loves us!"

I realized that day what Jesus did for me upon that cross.

Romans 5:8, "But God demonstrated His own love for us in this, while you were yet sinners, Christ died for us!"
Ezekiel 36:26, "I will give you a new heart and put a new spirit in you; I will remove from you your heart of stone and give you a heart of flesh."

Now what will you do with this love that you have been shown and given? Take it for granted or praise Him every day for what He has done? I hope and pray you respond the way I did in shouting, "OH HOW HE LOVES US!"

Chapter 8

Lost

To start out, this is a very humbling chapter to write. I travel a lot, and love to be on the road. A road trip, no matter how far, I'm usually in. In 2008, with traveling to festivals, random road trips and just driving to pick up kids around here for the skate park. Between the church van and my expedition at the time we totaled over 75,000 miles. That is absurd! That is a lot of hours on the road. This is a lot of gas, in the cars. This is tons of conversations and a few smelly vehicles. Now as a guy I would love to tell you that during those trips I never got lost once. Here is the thing, if I said that it would be a straight up lie. If you ever travel with me you know I am oblivious a lot of times while on the road and miss my exits many times. Honestly my sense of direction is horrible. Add in the fact that I get caught up in the music and talking and you are just asking to get lost. Some of those miles are due to me being lost. Now as a guy that is a humbling thing to admit. You may laugh or think I am being sarcastic but it truly is tough as a guy to admit that I get lost. I hate to stop and ask for directions. I would honestly rather drive around in circles for hours than admit to it. But through admitting it came some valuable life lessons for me about faith. Let me explain.

As part of this chapter I am going to pick on my mom and brother. They will help to prove my point. During the many hours on the road one of the two of them usually was with me, and Travis was actually with me when we made a cross country road trip circling the entire nation. He knows firsthand about my sense of direction.

So picture this, here I am driving and after about the fifth time passing the same sign and house on the right my mom starts to take notice and start saying, "Hey are you sure you know where you are going?" My first response when she says that is to turn up the volume and just ignore her. Then she starts to tap me on the shoulder and nagging me saying, "hey just stop, I will ask for directions and help you. "I continue driving. I don't want to admit the inevitable. Probably another hour goes by and the same sign and house over and over before I give in. "I'm lost." Ouch, that hurt to say, but within five minutes we are back on our way going in the right direction and of course I hear her say, "Now was that so hard to do, to let me help?" Yeah. In all reality it was, because I had to admit I needed help.

During the road trip Travis and I covered 9600 miles over twenty seven days. Starting in Pennsylvania we traveled west the whole way across the country to the west coast and San Francisco. From there we went up the coast through Oregon and Washington. Then we headed back east to Montana and Yellowstone National Park. Then we headed back south through Colorado down to Texas. After that we headed east to visit friends in Alabama and up the east coast. We did a figure eight of the country. What an experience! Honestly, without my brother, I would still probably be driving trying to find my way. Luckily though he is good with maps, and I am not just talking small fold up maps. I am talking the massive atlas that shows you everything.

Now you have to understand Travis is two years younger than me, and has always been smarter than me. He doesn't even open a book and still gets straight A's. Real smart! A humbling point for me was the fact that, I listened to my brother and allowed him to open the maps and look at where we were going to provide directions. Guess what, "Who would have ever thought that when you follow the maps it shows you where to go?"

Finally, was the GPS, with an annoying voice saying, "Recalculating, make a legal U-turn." I hated that thing and wanted to throw it out the window many times. If any of you have one, you know what I am talking about.

After all, that traveling though God really began to work on my heart showing me valuable life lessons through these experiences. All pretty simple life lessons, but ones that will stick with me the rest of my life and I hope will do the same for you.

He began by showing me that in life the first thing you have to admit is you are lost and need help. My mom in the passenger seat tapping me over and over is like Christ tapping at my heart, saying stop, admit you need help and I will guide you. You are lost because I am the way. As long as you keep trying to do things your own way, you will just continue to be frustrated and ending up in the same location. Yet that is exactly what I was doing. Until, Jesus got hold of my heart. I had to admit that I needed help. I had to stop seeking my own way and follow His way. Only then could I find my true direction in life. It took me admitting I was lost, seeking His help and allowing Him to guide me.

My brother with the road maps is like the Bible. We have direction to life found in God's word but we have to take the time to actually open it, to read it and to listen to it. God wants to provide direction to our life. As long as we just leave His word sitting on the shelves collecting dust it is no better than having maps in the pocket of our car seat. In Psalms 119, David writes the words, "Thy word is a lamp unto my feet and a light unto my path." Did you get that? God wants to light the path for you and show you how to live! But you have to stop, take the time to read it and allow him to lead you.

We would often rather try and find our own way, wandering through life searching and lost when we have God's road map and instructions right in front of us. Will we take the time to open it?

Finally, I had to learn that the GPS is like God's voice; recalculating, turn around, make a u-turn and repent! Do a 180! Through this I learned all about God's grace. Him saying, “You are never too lost for me!” “Listen to me.” “No matter how far off course you seem to be I will get you back on the path.” “You are never to gone for my love.” “No matter how far off you may seem, turn around, I am right here.” “Just listen to my voice and I will put you back on path.”

All these lessons start with the same thing for me and you. Admitting we need God's help. We’re not meant to do this life alone. That He will provide direction for us. I do not know how many people I have talked to who always have the same question, "How do I know God's direction for my life?" When I hear this question, my first response now to them is, "When was the last time you opened your Bible or spent time in prayer seeking Him?" The answer is usually pretty simple. Stop, Seek God, Open His word and follow him. As long as you continue to try and do this life on your own, you are always going to seem lost. True direction only comes from him!

Seems so simple, yet for some reason especially as guys we have a hard time doing that. We turn to our friends, then maybe even self-help books, then finally after all that fails we seek God.

God doesn't want us wandering through life feeling lost or confused, He wants to lead us!

Will you allow Him to lead you? Humble yourself, admit you're lost, and He will guide you.

Chapter 9

Go! Are You Willing?

What does it mean to go? Jesus' final command in Matthew 28 was to go, but what does that mean? Does that just refer to missions, like overseas? Or is that just a call for a special few? Or is that for all of us? For me I always thought it meant saying to God I will go to Africa or some other country, not back to Johnstown, my hometown. To be honest my dream always growing up was to get out of here as it is for most people. In life what I have come to find out the statement means making yourself willing and seeing where He leads you. That may sound like a pretty simplified version or even pretty obvious but let me expand.

In college I had no clue what God was calling me to do in life, but I do remember making the statement my sophomore year saying, "God I am willing." Next thing I knew one of the guys on my hall asked me to join him doing inner city ministry on Saturday mornings in the projects. For a few weeks I kept coming up with excuses. Inner city, I don't know how to relate. I am from Western Pennsylvania and like my country music. I don't know how to work with kids from there. Then, my excuses turned selfish, "But that is my time to sleep in each week." After a few weeks I would start waking up with God's conviction saying, "Are you willing?" "Of course I am God!" "Then no more excuses!"

I started going and you know what I found out. I fell in love with it. These inner city kids who I thought I could not connect with are just like every other kid out there. They want someone to hear their story and connect with them. They were just looking for someone to throw a football with and to pour their love into them. Through these experiences, this is how I honestly ended up in ministry. A few inner city kids moved my heart.

I got out of college with a youth ministry degree thinking I would jump into a church somewhere. God had other plans for me. I did do an internship at a local church while working at a snowboard shop. During my time at the snowboard shop I had the same type of experience in college, God saying,

"Go to the skaters in the area."

"But God, I can't skate."

"Are you willing?"

"Of Course, you know I am, but God I can't speak."

(So you know I just about failed speech class in college and really do not enjoy public speaking at all.)

"Are you willing?"

"But God, I…"

The excuses would continue until one day I was obedient and went armed with hot dogs and water. I had no clue, what I was getting myself into, only knowing that I told God I was willing. That summer at the local skate park God was faithful and began drawing kid's hearts to hear His word. The ministry grew from five to twenty kids. Now here is where it got crazy. You know outdoor parks around here close at Labor Day, so we started praying,

"God you have brought these 20 kids out, now what do we do?"

His response again, "Are you willing?"

Within two weeks we received a phone call of a local businessman who heard what we were doing and told us he had a building we could use. Praise God, He is faithful.

You think that is crazy, right? The story gets better. Five years ago, I was just turning twenty-five and ready to get a place of my own. I thought it was a good time to move out of my parents' home. I started looking in the paper for something suitable, nothing fancy. My eyes were glued right away to a listing. "You buy this house; you get a church with it." Wait, what, is this for real? No way! So we went and looked at it. It was real. Catholic Churches in the area were shutting and selling off their properties. The appraisers came in and told us the building is worth 2.1 million dollars. "God I can't afford that." "Again, let me remind you I work at a snowboard shop, no way." "Are you willing?" But again God is faithful! Church and the house combined was worth that much, but they were only asking fifty two thousand dollars. No way, did I hear you right? "Worth 2.1 million dollars and only asking 52 thousand dollars?" That just doesn't make sense. So I started the Crucified Church!

Throughout the last seven years God had continued to do things like these two stories. He has continually blown us away with His faithfulness. The church is now one of the only college ministries in town and the skate park is the only indoor park in the area, still free of charge to kids. Both are meeting needs that were in the area. God knew what He was doing. We just had to make ourselves willing and allow Him to do the work. None of it is what I had ever envisioned with my life, but He had other plans.

I ask you now, when God says go, Are you willing? You never know what that is going to look like or how it is going to turn out, but he is faithful and when He calls you to something He will provide.

There is no doubt in my mind that God has been convicting some of your hearts to go. Have

you been coming up with excuses? No more excuses. There is really one question to ask yourself.

Are you willing? If your answer is yes, than just trust Him and watch what He does.

Chapter 10

ShowTime

James 4:14, “You’re are a mist that appears for a little while and then vanishes."

This is one of those verses I have read over many times in life, but it was not until the last few years that it has really hit me just how true it is. Our lives are but a vapor that could be here today and gone tomorrow. Working with kids has really made me think about that and hopefully will make you think. Here is why.

Let me paint an image in your mind to start this chapter off. Here we are a group of twelve in Washington D.C. skating at the Freedom Plaza. It is about ninety five degrees outside with a bright blue sky. Let me just say it was a perfect day we were completely carefree. We were taking in the moments that you remember in life. Around one o’clock or so we all decide to take a break for lunch and gather up when we start to hear some commotion off in the distance. Like anyone would do we start to pay attention. What we notice though was heartbreaking. Three businessmen dressed in their finest making fun of an obvious homeless man, mocking him, spitting on him and causing problems. He was wearing a North Carolina starter winter jacket in the middle of this heat and carrying around three massive garbage bags, as well as a paper bags for hiding his alcohol. Let me say this, “I was proud of the way the skaters handled it, not joining in, but actually showing concern for this guy.”

The next thing we know he notices us and starts making his way towards us. Stumbling a little bit he begins to put his hand up to his mouth with his pointer and finger raised and starts to whisper, "It's Showtime." At first we are taken back a little bit because he just keeps whispering this statement. He doesn't come over asking for money or a handout but just wants someone to talk to. Here we are and we begin to listen to his story. He starts out by asking us if we had ever been to Arizona. "No," we all reply. He replies, "Good cuz I rob banks there." With that statement we all just keep listening wondering what he is talking about. Then he begins to say Showtime again. Only this time he is telling us that Showtime is his name and that he got that name from friends who knew him in Arizona. The story would continue on for probably fifteen more minutes with the idea that when it came to robbing banks he had eight minutes to get in and get out before the police would show up. For eight minutes, that was his Showtime. If he didn't finish he would be busted so he had to make the most of that time. He shared of the idea that he had like a mental clock telling just how much time he had. I will never forget that day or that encounter. I am sure the guys who were with me would probably say the same thing.

After "Showtime" left us that day we all just sat back trying to take in what we had just experienced. What came out of it I would have never imagined. We talked about the idea of how would we live if we all knew exactly how much time we had to live? Like a clock in front of us counting down our moments. Showtime knew he had eight minutes.

Really think about this thought. What if I told you, you had one year left? Dave you have eight years. Tom you have seventy-two years. Mike you have three days. What if we could literally keep a tab on how much time we had left? Would we change how we lived? The conversations we have? The choices we would make? If you are like me I can almost guarantee each and every one of us would say yes to that question. Here is the thing though, we do not have that clock in front of us, so we must learn to make the most of every moment before our clock runs out. Are there things you would change? "Would you try skydiving or rocky mountain climbing?" I went two point seven seconds on a bull named Fumanchu!" Recently, movies have come out all about the things you want to do before you kick the bucket. Yet so many times we just look at that idea and say, "I have a ton of life left to live." But what if you don't? It is not a guarantee, but a vapor.

What about your words and conversations with others? This idea never hit me so hard until this past summer when one of our bikers from the skate park drown while trying to swim across a local river. Going into that day I can guarantee you he never thought that it would be his final moments. This kid was so full of life with so many big dreams to live. The joy and hope I can now find in writing this chapter is the fact that I know without a doubt he is in heaven right now celebrating with his Savior and is way better off. I can tell you this because throughout the three years before him I would give him a ride to the skate park on a weekly basis and know where he stood in his faith. What a blessing! I now carry around the card from his funeral in my car with the statement written on it, make every conversation count! What if I hadn't taken the time to have those conversations and instead just talked sports, weather and about other things with him? Would I regret that time that we had? Would I question his fate?

What about all the other conversations we have though? What about those closest to us? What about when we walk out the door angry at our parents? What if something would happen to them? I remember having a conversation with a local kid here whose dad passed away and his regret is that his final talk with his dad was in anger. Now he wishes so bad he could take that back. The last few years were very tough on him, but I am glad to say that he worked through it and now lives by his dad's favorite saying, "Run every race like it is your last and live every day like it could be your last."

I am not writing this chapter to give kids a reason to go buck wild like the new motto YOLO. I am writing this chapter to tell you that you never know how much time you have. We should live in a way that we desire to bring God glory every day of our lives. We need to make our lives a “SHOWTIME” for Him. What is He calling you to do? Are you going to follow after Him, seeking him daily, saying, "God what do you have for me now?" My worry is that when we stand before Him one day, many will make the statement, "God, I just thought I had more time!"

Make every day count! Make every conversation count! Make your life count!

James 4:14, "You are a mist that appears for a little while and then vanishes."

Chapter 11

A Dangerous Prayer, a Serious Calling

Let me start out this chapter by saying I hope you are serious about your faith and to really think about it. Are ready for what God has in store? I found this out personally in my life two summers ago. I have never been the same since and have seen a shakeup in my own life, in my brother's life, in the church and also in the way I now worship. Let's go back two years. It was the summer of 2011 and my travel season was winding down. I had just gotten home from New Hampshire with the skate team from Soul fest. I was pretty amped about what God was doing. It was a Sunday Night at church and one of our leaders came up and just asked me the simple question, "What do you have going on this week?" My response was pretty simple, "Well I just plan on recovering from the last week." "Why's that?" He went on to tell me how he had volunteered to drive a car to California for a girl in college out there that he knew.

As I have told you I love to travel, so without much thought I was in. My simple question for him was, "when do we leave?" "Tuesday," he said. Perfect, I didn't even unpack my bag; I just threw it in the car and was good to go. One day of rest, on the road again. Now to remind you I live in Pennsylvania, so a trip to California is a good thirty six hours. This would be a lot of time in the car to think, write, pray and just chill. I was excited, Venice Beach, Pinks Hot Dogs, Hollywood, and the beach. "Heck yeah!" So I thought...

Needless to say this trip changed my life or I wouldn't be writing about it. So you know the guy I traveled with is one of the few guys in my life that when we get together we just begin to feed off each other's faith. Like straight up preaching in the car. If someone drove by us they would probably crack up laughing, because we are both loud and egg each other on to the point that when we get out we are like Peter and John in Acts, going you cannot keep me silent. And this went on for most of the trip. I had no clue what I was in store for. As we started he told me how he had made a few phone calls and that once we got out to L.A. we not only would be dropping off the car but we would spend a few days working at the Dream Center, on Skid Row and passing out food to the homeless . Not quite the beach, but sounded legit to me.

By the time we got there we were fired up. I am not sure if it was all the caffeine in my system from energy drinks and coffee, feeding off the passion of each-other, or God preparing us for what was in store, but the next seventy two hours were unforgettable. The first day we went and worked the food truck passing out who knows how much food to the homeless around L.A. Hours upon hours of people lining up to just get food to last them throughout the day. I believe they said they pass out about a million pounds of food. Incredible! Not only do they pass it out but every morning when it comes in, the volunteers at the Dream Center have to sort through it to send out to different locations. I will never forget getting off the truck that first stop and seeing people lined up for food.

The next morning was probably the most heartbreaking. We got to go and experience Skid Row. I had heard rumors and read stories about it but nothing could have prepared me for some of the things we encountered that day. They prepared us the best they could and made sure to repeat for us not to wander off on our own. They also told us not to give out our actual name, phone number, and to make sure we didn't have any valuables in our possession. I was pretty naive and thought that it couldn't be that bad. After all, I had worked with homeless in Baltimore before. Not to gross you out, but to give you a picture my job that day was to go around and try to pick up as much trash and garbage from around that I could. Sounded, pretty straight up, right? So, here I went with a group of four others armed with garbage bags, rubber gloves, a dust pan and two push brooms. It was time to bring back some dignity to these people and show them the love of Christ. I didn't realize that meant picking up dirty syringes, sweeping up feces', used condoms and straight up filth. My heart began to break realizing the conditions some of these people had to live in. One of the members of our team actually had to walk away from getting sick from the smells and sights. Throughout the day I got to actually hear a few of the men and women tell their stories.

First was a guy in his mid forties. At first glance I would have definitely thought he was in his sixties at least from how ragged and beat up he looked. He began to share of how he used to make six figures as an engineer, how he was married at one time and how he used to live. But then he shared how when the economy crashed he lost his job, his wife left him and he ended up bankrupt and here on the streets. You could tell all hope had been taken away after being out here for so long. Next was a woman who shared how dangerous it is for her being out here and that rape was a common thing because the police have pretty much given up trying to do anything to protect the homeless. Finally the person who sticks out in my mind was a complete addict who told me that he would do anything just to get a fix. You could have offered this guy a home, a job, a fresh start, but he would choose to stay here just to get his fix.

At the end of the day I had a hard time even going back to the hotel and looking at the possessions I had with me knowing the conditions of what I just had experienced. Even that night, I struggled sleeping thinking about that man who had it all and is now on the street. My heart was breaking and God was beginning to work in my heart. I talked to Jeremy and he was feeling the same way. We couldn't believe that we would be flying back to Pennsylvania soon and to our normal everyday comfortable lives. That night and the next few days we began to pray one of the most dangerous prayers I know. Our prayer was simple, "God, if people like this exist back in Johnstown, open my eyes to them. Jesus, Let me not turn a blind eye to those in need."

Let me tell you my eyes were opened! God began to allow me to see things I had never seen before. We got back to Johnstown and started to share our stories of what we experienced and next thing you knew we would be getting involved in a homeless and broken dinner in town that feeds about forty to forty-five a week. We started hearing the stories of people in our own small town who experienced or went thru some of the same things as those people on Skid Row. Not quite the thousands of L.A., but it was a start. Next thing I knew God began to open my heart and eyes to the broken in Central Park as I drove by on a daily basis. How had I been blind to them for so long? How could I not see these people in their need for so many years? Had I been blind to them or honestly just not want to see it?

The following week at church I actually started focusing more on the words of the worship songs we were singing, "Break my heart for what breaks yours," and "I will go, I will go, I will go, Lord send me." These words had such new meaning to me. While singing them I began crying as I thought about if I was serious about working with the broken, the homeless, the beat-up and the hurting. God was convicting my heart again saying, "Only sing these words if you actually mean them." I had a decision to make. Step up or Shut up as my brother likes to say. God will open your eyes and send you, but are you willing and that was a question I had to ask myself that day. Let me tell you two years later, my life has never been the same! Getting to know the stories of people in my town has brought me joy, heartache, peace, and pain. I believe overall this has brought me closer to the heart of Christ!

How about you? When you see the homeless and hurting do you just turn a blind eye? When you sing those lyrics are you ready for what they mean or do they just feel good to say? God is calling you and wants to open your eyes to the reality of people around you, but do you really want to see it? Do you really want to experience the heart of Christ? Or are you comfortable in your pew focused on your own issues, that you are missing what is actually taking place in the world around you?

I promise you this. If you begin to pray God open my eyes and break my heart, He will. Your life will never be the same. It is not easy, and working with some of these people is challenging. The rewards are so worth it when you get to know them. Who knows, they could turn out to be some of your best friends.

For my brother this meant moving to Haiti. For our church it has meant providing housing, food, clothes, and someone to talk to. For me it has meant learning to live on the basic necessities and giving most of what I have away. My heart has been forever changed and I pray now as I finish writing this book that your heart would be convicted and your life will be forever changed.

Religion that God our Father accepts as pure and faultless is this: to look after orphans and widows in their distress... James 1:27

Are you ready? This book has discussed how Jesus works outside the walls of church. I hope that you take it personally. Go and watch what He does in your life. He may surprise you. Honestly, He may call you to a life you never expected!

Bibliography

Barker, Kenneth, Gen. Ed. The NIV Study Bible, Grand Rapids, MI: Zondervan, 1995 Crossway Bibles.

Web Sites:

Josh Knipple Http:// www.crucifiedministries.com

Publisher Site Http:// www.abbafathermedia.com

About The Author

Josh Knipple has been in ministry for seven years in many different roles. He runs a local skate park and a church known as Crucified. He loves to travel, speak, and go on mission's trips and anything in between to share his passion for Christ. His home base is Johnstown Pennsylvania, but any given day who knows where you might run into him.